MznLnx

Missing Links Exam Preps

Exam Prep for

Supervision in the Hospitality Industry

Kavanaugh & Ninemeier, 4th Edition

The MznLnx Exam Prep is your link from the texbook and lecture to your exams.
The MznLnx Exam Preps are unauthorized and comprehensive reviews of your textbooks.

All material provided by MznLnx and Rico Publications (c) 2010
Textbook publishers and textbook authors do not particpate in or contribute to these reviews.

MznLnx

Rico
Publications

Exam Prep for Supervision in the Hospitality Industry
4th Edition
Kavanaugh & Ninemeier

Publisher: Raymond Houge
Assistant Editor: Michael Rouger
Text and Cover Designer: Lisa Buckner
Marketing Manager: Sara Swagger
Project Manager, Editorial Production: Jerry Emerson
Art Director: Vernon Lowerui

Product Manager: Dave Mason
Editorial Asitant: Rachel Guzmanji
Pedagogy: Debra Long
Cover Image: Jim Reed/Getty Images
Text and Cover Printer: City Printing, Inc.
Compositor: Media Mix, Inc.

(c) 2010 Rico Publications
ALL RIGHTS RESERVED. No part of this work covered by the copyright may be reproduced or used in any form or by an means--graphic, electronic, or mechanical, including photocopying, recording, taping, Web distribution, information storage, and retrieval systems, or in any other manner--without the written permission of the publisher.

Printed in the United States
ISBN:

For more information about our products, contact us at:
Dave.Mason@RicoPublications.com

For permission to use material from this text or product, submit a request online to:
Dave.Mason@RicoPublications.com

Contents

CHAPTER 1
The Supervisor and the Management Process 1

CHAPTER 2
Effective Communication 7

CHAPTER 3
Recruitment and Selection Procedures 10

CHAPTER 4
Training and Orientation 15

CHAPTER 5
Managing Productivity and Controlling Labor Costs 20

CHAPTER 6
Evaluating and Coaching 25

CHAPTER 7
Discipline 30

CHAPTER 8
Special Supervisory Concerns 33

CHAPTER 9
Team Building 40

CHAPTER 10
Motivation Through Leadership 44

CHAPTER 11
Managing Conflict 49

CHAPTER 12
Time Management 51

CHAPTER 13
Managing Change 53

CHAPTER 14
Professional Development 55

ANSWER KEY 58

TO THE STUDENT

COMPREHENSIVE

The *MznLnx* Exam Prep series is designed to help you pass your exams. Editors at MznLnx review your textbooks and then prepare these practice exams to help you master the textbook material. Unlike study guides, workbooks, and practice tests provided by the texbook publisher and textbook authors, *MznLnx* gives you **all** of the material in each chapter in exam form, not just samples, so you can be sure to nail your exam.

MECHANICAL

The MznLnx Exam Prep series creates exams that will help you learn the subject matter as well as test you on your understanding. Each question is designed to help you master the concept. Just working through the exams, you gain an understanding of the subject--its a simple mechanical process that produces success.

INTEGRATED STUDY GUIDE AND REVIEW

MznLnx is not just a set of exams designed to test you, its also a comprehensive review of the subject content. Each exam question is also a review of the concept, making sure that you will get the answer correct without having to go to other sources of material. You learn as you go! Its the easiest way to pass an exam.

HUMOR

Studying can be tedious and dry. MznLnx's instructional design includes moderate humor within the exam questions on occassion, to break the tedium and revitalize the brain

Chapter 1. The Supervisor and the Management Process

1. The _____ of 1990 (ADA) is the short title of United States (Pub.L. 101-336, 104 Stat. 327, enacted July 26, 1990), codified at 42 U.S.C. § 12101 et seq. It was signed into law on July 26, 1990, by President George H. W. Bush, and later amended with changes effective January 1, 2009. The ADA is a wide-ranging civil rights law that prohibits, under certain circumstances, discrimination based on disability. It affords similar protections against discrimination to Americans with disabilities as the Civil Rights Act of 1964,
   a. Australian labour law
   b. Americans with Disabilities Act
   c. Employment discrimination
   d. Equal Pay Act of 1963

2. _____ is a term used to describe a policy of allowing events to take their own course. The term is a French phrase literally meaning 'let do'. It is a doctrine that states that government generally should not intervene in the marketplace.
   a. Freedom of contract
   b. Libertarian
   c. Deep ecology
   d. Laissez-faire

3. In business and accounting, _____s are everything of value that is owned by a person or company. Any property or object of value that one possesses, usually considered as applicable to the payment of one's debts is considered an _____. Simplistically stated, _____s are things of value that can be readily converted into cash.
   a. A Stake in the Outcome
   b. A4e
   c. Asset
   d. AAAI

4. _____ has been described as the 'process of social influence in which one person can enlist the aid and support of others in the accomplishment of a common task' . A definition more inclusive of followers comes from Alan Keith of Genentech who said '_____ is ultimately about creating a way for people to contribute to making something extraordinary happen.'

   _____ is one of the most salient aspects of the organizational context. However, defining _____ has been challenging.

   a. Situational leadership
   b. 28-hour day
   c. 1990 Clean Air Act
   d. Leadership

Chapter 1. The Supervisor and the Management Process

5. _____ occurs when expectant women are fired, not hired, or otherwise discriminated against due to their pregnancy or intention to become pregnant. Common forms of _____ include not being hired due to visible pregnancy or likelihood of becoming pregnant, being fired after informing an employer of one's pregnancy, being fired after maternity leave, and receiving a pay dock due to pregnancy. In the United States, since 1978, employers are legally bound to provide what insurance, leave pay, and additional support that would be bestowed upon any employee with medical leave or disability.
   a. 1990 Clean Air Act
   b. 33 Strategies of War
   c. 28-hour day
   d. Pregnancy Discrimination

6. The _____ was a landmark piece of legislation in the United States that outlawed racial segregation in schools, public places, and employment.
   a. Financial Security Law of France
   b. Negligence in employment
   c. Civil Rights Act of 1964
   d. Design patent

7. _____ is the process by which the activities of an organisation, particularly those regarding decision-making, become concentrated within a particular location and/or group.
   a. Product innovation
   b. Corner office
   c. Chief operating officer
   d. Centralization

8. _____ is a cross-disciplinary area concerned with protecting the safety, health and welfare of people engaged in work or employment. The goal of all _____ programs is to foster a work free safe environment. As a secondary effect, it may also protect co-workers, family members, employers, customers, suppliers, nearby communities, and other members of the public who are impacted by the workplace environment.
   a. AAAI
   b. A4e
   c. A Stake in the Outcome
   d. Occupational Safety and Health

9. The United States _____ is an agency of the United States Department of Labor. It was created by Congress under the Occupational Safety and Health Act, signed by President Richard M. Nixon, on December 29, 1970. Its mission is to prevent work-related injuries, illnesses, and deaths by issuing and enforcing rules (called standards) for workplace safety and health.

a. Unemployment insurance
b. Opinion leadership
c. Operant conditioning
d. Occupational Safety and Health Administration

10. An _____ is a subset of strategic work plan. It describes short-term ways of achieving milestones and explains how, or what portion of, a strategic plan will be put into operation during a given operational period, in the case of commercial application, a fiscal year or another given budgetary term. An operational plan is the basis for, and justification of an annual operating budget request.
   a. A Stake in the Outcome
   b. A4e
   c. Operational planning
   d. AAAI

11. _____ is an organization's process of defining its strategy and making decisions on allocating its resources to pursue this strategy, including its capital and people. Various business analysis techniques can be used in _____, including SWOT analysis (Strengths, Weaknesses, Opportunities, and Threats) and PEST analysis (Political, Economic, Social, and Technological analysis) or STEER analysis involving Socio-cultural, Technological, Economic, Ecological, and Regulatory factors and EPISTEL (Environment, Political, Informatic, Social, Technological, Economic and Legal)

_____ is the formal consideration of an organization's future course. All _____ deals with at least one of three key questions:

   1. 'What do we do?'
   2. 'For whom do we do it?'
   3. 'How do we excel?'

In business _____, the third question is better phrased 'How can we beat or avoid competition?'. (Bradford and Duncan, page 1.)

   a. Strategic planning
   b. 33 Strategies of War
   c. 28-hour day
   d. 1990 Clean Air Act

12. _____ generally refers to a list of all planned expenses and revenues. It is a plan for saving and spending. A _____ is an important concept in microeconomics, which uses a _____ line to illustrate the trade-offs between two or more goods.

a. 28-hour day
b. 1990 Clean Air Act
c. 33 Strategies of War
d. Budget

13. A _____ is a formal statement of a set of business goals, the reasons why they are believed attainable, and the plan for reaching those goals. It may also contain background information about the organization or team attempting to reach those goals.

The business goals may be defined for for-profit or for non-profit organizations.

   a. Crisis management
   b. Distributed management
   c. Time management
   d. Business plan

14. _____ is an integrated communications-based process through which individuals and communities discover that existing and newly-identified needs and wants may be satisfied by the products and services of others.

_____ is defined by the American _____ Association as the activity, set of institutions, and processes for creating, communicating, delivering, and exchanging offerings that have value for customers, clients, partners, and society at large. The term developed from the original meaning which referred literally to going to market, as in shopping, or going to a market to buy or sell goods or services.

   a. Customer relationship management
   b. Market development
   c. Marketing
   d. Disruptive technology

15. A _____ is a written document that details the necessary actions to achieve one or more marketing objectives. It can be for a product or service, a brand, or a product line. _____s cover between one and five years.
   a. Marketing plan
   b. Marketing strategy
   c. Disruptive technology
   d. Market development

16. _____ is one of the managerial functions like planning, organizing, staffing and directing. It is an important function because it helps to check the errors and to take the corrective action so that deviation from standards are minimized and stated goals of the organization are achieved in desired manner. According to modern concepts, _____ is a foreseeing action whereas earlier concept of _____ was used only when errors were detected. _____ in management means setting standards, measuring actual performance and taking corrective action.
   a. Schedule of reinforcement
   b. Turnover
   c. Decision tree pruning
   d. Control

17. A _____ is a list of the general tasks and responsibilities of a position. Typically, it also includes to whom the position reports, specifications such as the qualifications needed by the person in the job, salary range for the position, etc. A _____ is usually developed by conducting a job analysis, which includes examining the tasks and sequences of tasks necessary to perform the job.
   a. Recruitment advertising
   b. Job description
   c. Recruitment Process Insourcing
   d. Recruitment

18. _____ Movement refers to those researchers of organizational development who study the behavior of people in groups, in particular workplace groups. It originated in the 1920s' Hawthorne studies, which examined the effects of social relations, motivation and employee satisfaction on factory productivity. The movement viewed workers in terms of their psychology and fit with companies, rather than as interchangeable parts.
   a. Human relations
   b. Participatory management
   c. Work design
   d. Hersey-Blanchard situational theory

19. In economics, business, retail, and accounting, a _____ is the value of money that has been used up to produce something, and hence is not available for use anymore. In economics, a _____ is an alternative that is given up as a result of a decision. In business, the _____ may be one of acquisition, in which case the amount of money expended to acquire it is counted as _____.
   a. Cost overrun
   b. Cost
   c. Cost allocation
   d. Fixed costs

20. _____ is a structured approach to transitioning individuals, teams, and organizations from a current state to a desired future state. The current definition of _____ includes both organizational _____ processes and individual _____ models, which together are used to manage the people side of change.

A number of models are available for understanding the transitioning of individuals through the phases of _____ and strengthening organizational development initiative in both government and corporate sectors.

a. 28-hour day
b. Change management
c. 33 Strategies of War
d. 1990 Clean Air Act

Chapter 2. Effective Communication

1. The _____ was a landmark piece of legislation in the United States that outlawed racial segregation in schools, public places, and employment.
   a. Negligence in employment
   b. Design patent
   c. Financial Security Law of France
   d. Civil Rights Act of 1964

2. _____ is a term used to describe a policy of allowing events to take their own course. The term is a French phrase literally meaning 'let do'. It is a doctrine that states that government generally should not intervene in the marketplace.
   a. Deep ecology
   b. Libertarian
   c. Freedom of contract
   d. Laissez-faire

3. _____ has been described as the 'process of social influence in which one person can enlist the aid and support of others in the accomplishment of a common task' . A definition more inclusive of followers comes from Alan Keith of Genentech who said '_____ is ultimately about creating a way for people to contribute to making something extraordinary happen.'

   _____ is one of the most salient aspects of the organizational context. However, defining _____ has been challenging.

   a. Situational leadership
   b. 1990 Clean Air Act
   c. Leadership
   d. 28-hour day

4. The _____ 1970 is an Act of the United Kingdom Parliament which prohibits any less favourable treatment between men and women in terms of pay and conditions of employment. It came into force on 29 December 1975. The term pay is interpreted in a broad sense to include, on top of wages, things like holidays, pension rights, company perks and some kinds of bonuses.
   a. Architectural Barriers Act of 1968
   b. Oncale v. Sundowner Offshore Services
   c. Australian labour law
   d. Equal Pay Act

Chapter 2. Effective Communication

5. The _____, Pub. L. No. 88-38, 77 Stat. 56, (June 10, 1963) codified at 29 U.S.C. Â§ 206(d), is a United States federal law amending the Fair Labor Standards Act, aimed at abolishing wage differentials based on sex. In passing the bill, Congress denounces sex discrimination.
   a. Architectural Barriers Act of 1968
   b. Equal Pay Act of 1963
   c. Extra time
   d. Invitee

6. _____ occurs when expectant women are fired, not hired, or otherwise discriminated against due to their pregnancy or intention to become pregnant. Common forms of _____ include not being hired due to visible pregnancy or likelihood of becoming pregnant, being fired after informing an employer of one's pregnancy, being fired after maternity leave, and receiving a pay dock due to pregnancy. In the United States, since 1978, employers are legally bound to provide what insurance, leave pay, and additional support that would be bestowed upon any employee with medical leave or disability.
   a. 33 Strategies of War
   b. 1990 Clean Air Act
   c. 28-hour day
   d. Pregnancy Discrimination

7. _____ is a cross-disciplinary area concerned with protecting the safety, health and welfare of people engaged in work or employment. The goal of all _____ programs is to foster a work free safe environment. As a secondary effect, it may also protect co-workers, family members, employers, customers, suppliers, nearby communities, and other members of the public who are impacted by the workplace environment.
   a. Occupational Safety and Health
   b. AAAI
   c. A Stake in the Outcome
   d. A4e

8. The United States _____ is an agency of the United States Department of Labor. It was created by Congress under the Occupational Safety and Health Act, signed by President Richard M. Nixon, on December 29, 1970. Its mission is to prevent work-related injuries, illnesses, and deaths by issuing and enforcing rules (called standards) for workplace safety and health.
   a. Unemployment insurance
   b. Opinion leadership
   c. Occupational Safety and Health Administration
   d. Operant conditioning

Chapter 2. Effective Communication

9. The _____ refers to a cognitive bias whereby the perception of a particular trait is influenced by the perception of the former traits in a sequence of interpretations.

Edward L. Thorndike was the first to support the _____ with empirical research. In a psychology study published in 1920, Thorndike asked commanding officers to rate their soldiers; Thorndike found high cross-correlation between all positive and all negative traits.

   a. Cognitive biases
   b. Sunk costs
   c. Halo effect
   d. Distinction bias

10. _____ is both the conscious and unconscious act of revealing more about ourselves to others. This may include but is not limited to thoughts, feelings, aspirations, goals, failures, successes, fears, dreams as well as our likes, dislikes, and favorites. Many people attempt to avoid 'self-disclosing' too much to coworkers, or when dating for fear of being judged negatively by others.
   a. Social influence
   b. Soft skill
   c. Social network analysis
   d. Self-disclosure

11. _____ is one of the managerial functions like planning, organizing, staffing and directing. It is an important function because it helps to check the errors and to take the corrective action so that deviation from standards are minimized and stated goals of the organization are achieved in desired manner. According to modern concepts, _____ is a foreseeing action whereas earlier concept of _____ was used only when errors were detected. _____ in management means setting standards, measuring actual performance and taking corrective action.
   a. Turnover
   b. Schedule of reinforcement
   c. Control
   d. Decision tree pruning

Chapter 3. Recruitment and Selection Procedures

1. _____ is a term used to describe a policy of allowing events to take their own course. The term is a French phrase literally meaning 'let do'. It is a doctrine that states that government generally should not intervene in the marketplace.
    a. Libertarian
    b. Freedom of contract
    c. Laissez-faire
    d. Deep ecology

2. _____ is an increasingly broadening term with which an organization, or other human system describes the combination of traditionally administrative personnel functions with acquisition and application of skills, knowledge and experience, Employee Relations and resource planning at various levels. The field draws upon concepts developed in Industrial/Organizational Psychology and System Theory. _____ has at least two related interpretations depending on context. The original usage derives from political economy and economics, where it was traditionally called labor, one of four factors of production although this perspective is changing as a function of new and ongoing research into more strategic approaches at national levels. This first usage is used more in terms of '_____ development', and can go beyond just organizations to the level of nations . The more traditional usage within corporations and businesses refers to the individuals within a firm or agency, and to the portion of the organization that deals with hiring, firing, training, and other personnel issues, typically referred to as `_____ management'.
    a. Human resource management
    b. Bradford Factor
    c. Progressive discipline
    d. Human resources

3. _____ has been described as the 'process of social influence in which one person can enlist the aid and support of others in the accomplishment of a common task' . A definition more inclusive of followers comes from Alan Keith of Genentech who said '_____ is ultimately about creating a way for people to contribute to making something extraordinary happen.'

    _____ is one of the most salient aspects of the organizational context. However, defining _____ has been challenging.

    a. Situational leadership
    b. Leadership
    c. 1990 Clean Air Act
    d. 28-hour day

4. _____ is one of the managerial functions like planning, organizing, staffing and directing. It is an important function because it helps to check the errors and to take the corrective action so that deviation from standards are minimized and stated goals of the organization are achieved in desired manner.According to modern concepts, _____ is a foreseeing action whereas earlier concept of _____ was used only when errors were detected. _____ in management means setting standards, measuring actual performance and taking corrective action.

Chapter 3. Recruitment and Selection Procedures

a. Schedule of reinforcement
b. Turnover
c. Decision tree pruning
d. Control

5. _____ occurs when expectant women are fired, not hired, or otherwise discriminated against due to their pregnancy or intention to become pregnant. Common forms of _____ include not being hired due to visible pregnancy or likelihood of becoming pregnant, being fired after informing an employer of one's pregnancy, being fired after maternity leave, and receiving a pay dock due to pregnancy. In the United States, since 1978, employers are legally bound to provide what insurance, leave pay, and additional support that would be bestowed upon any employee with medical leave or disability.
   a. 1990 Clean Air Act
   b. 28-hour day
   c. Pregnancy Discrimination
   d. 33 Strategies of War

6. A _____ is a list of the general tasks and responsibilities of a position. Typically, it also includes to whom the position reports, specifications such as the qualifications needed by the person in the job, salary range for the position, etc. A _____ is usually developed by conducting a job analysis, which includes examining the tasks and sequences of tasks necessary to perform the job.
   a. Recruitment
   b. Recruitment Process Insourcing
   c. Recruitment advertising
   d. Job description

7. The _____ was a landmark piece of legislation in the United States that outlawed racial segregation in schools, public places, and employment.
   a. Negligence in employment
   b. Financial Security Law of France
   c. Design patent
   d. Civil Rights Act of 1964

8. The _____ 1970 is an Act of the United Kingdom Parliament which prohibits any less favourable treatment between men and women in terms of pay and conditions of employment. It came into force on 29 December 1975. The term pay is interpreted in a broad sense to include, on top of wages, things like holidays, pension rights, company perks and some kinds of bonuses.

Chapter 3. Recruitment and Selection Procedures

   a. Architectural Barriers Act of 1968
   b. Equal Pay Act
   c. Oncale v. Sundowner Offshore Services
   d. Australian labour law

9. The _____, Pub. L. No. 88-38, 77 Stat. 56, (June 10, 1963) codified at 29 U.S.C. Â§ 206(d), is a United States federal law amending the Fair Labor Standards Act, aimed at abolishing wage differentials based on sex. In passing the bill, Congress denounces sex discrimination.
   a. Architectural Barriers Act of 1968
   b. Extra time
   c. Invitee
   d. Equal Pay Act of 1963

10. In a human resources context, _____ or labor _____ is the rate at which an employer gains and loses employees. Simple ways to describe it are 'how long employees tend to stay' or 'the rate of traffic through the revolving door.' _____ is measured for individual companies and for their industry as a whole. If an employer is said to have a high _____ relative to its competitors, it means that employees of that company have a shorter average tenure than those of other companies in the same industry.
   a. Continuous
   b. Career portfolios
   c. Turnover
   d. Ten year occupational employment projection

11. An _____ is an interview conducted by an employer of a departing employee. They are generally conducted by a relatively neutral party, such as a human resources staff member, so that the employee will be more inclined to be candid, as opposed to worrying about burning bridges. For this reason, some companies opt to employ a third party to conduct the interviews and provide feedback.
   a. Underemployment
   b. Occupational Employment Statistics
   c. Extra role performance
   d. Exit interview

12. The _____ of 1990 (ADA) is the short title of United States (Pub.L. 101-336, 104 Stat. 327, enacted July 26, 1990), codified at 42 U.S.C. Â§ 12101 et seq. It was signed into law on July 26, 1990, by President George H. W. Bush, and later amended with changes effective January 1, 2009. The ADA is a wide-ranging civil rights law that prohibits, under certain circumstances, discrimination based on disability. It affords similar protections against discrimination to Americans with disabilities as the Civil Rights Act of 1964,

a. Australian labour law
b. Equal Pay Act of 1963
c. Employment discrimination
d. Americans with Disabilities Act

13. _____ is a term defined by the Oxford English Dictionary as an individual's 'course or progress through life '. It is usually considered to pertain to remunerative work (and sometimes also formal education.)

The etymology of the term is somewhat ironic in that it comes from the Latin word carrera, which means race .

a. Spatial mismatch
b. Nursing shortage
c. Career planning
d. Career

14. In employment law, a (BFOQ) (US) or bona fide occupational requirement (BFOR) (Canada) is a quality or an attribute that employers are allowed to consider when making decisions on the hiring and retention of employees - qualities that, when considered, in other contexts would be considered discriminatory and thus violating civil rights employment law.

In employment discrimination law in the United States, United States Code Title 29 , Chapter 14 (age discrimination in employment), section 623 (prohibition of age discrimination) establishes that 'It shall not be unlawful for an employer, employment agency, or labor organization (1) to take any action otherwise prohibited under subsections (a), (b), (c), or (e) of this section where age is a _____ reasonably necessary to the normal operation of the particular business, or where the differentiation is based on reasonable factors other than age, or where such practices involve an employee in a workplace in a foreign country, and compliance with such subsections would cause such employer, or a corporation controlled by such employer, to violate the laws of the country in which such workplace is located.'

One example of _____s are mandatory retirement ages for bus drivers and airline pilots, for safety reasons. Further, in advertising, a manufacturer of men's clothing may lawfully advertise for male models.

a. Corporate governance
b. Bona fide occupational qualification
c. Sick leave
d. MacPherson v. Buick Motor Co.

Chapter 3. Recruitment and Selection Procedures

15. _____ is a cross-disciplinary area concerned with protecting the safety, health and welfare of people engaged in work or employment. The goal of all _____ programs is to foster a work free safe environment. As a secondary effect, it may also protect co-workers, family members, employers, customers, suppliers, nearby communities, and other members of the public who are impacted by the workplace environment.
   a. Occupational Safety and Health
   b. A Stake in the Outcome
   c. AAAI
   d. A4e

16. The United States _____ is an agency of the United States Department of Labor. It was created by Congress under the Occupational Safety and Health Act, signed by President Richard M. Nixon, on December 29, 1970. Its mission is to prevent work-related injuries, illnesses, and deaths by issuing and enforcing rules (called standards) for workplace safety and health.
   a. Operant conditioning
   b. Occupational Safety and Health Administration
   c. Unemployment insurance
   d. Opinion leadership

Chapter 4. Training and Orientation

1. The _____ 1970 is an Act of the United Kingdom Parliament which prohibits any less favourable treatment between men and women in terms of pay and conditions of employment. It came into force on 29 December 1975. The term pay is interpreted in a broad sense to include, on top of wages, things like holidays, pension rights, company perks and some kinds of bonuses.
    a. Architectural Barriers Act of 1968
    b. Oncale v. Sundowner Offshore Services
    c. Australian labour law
    d. Equal Pay Act

2. The _____, Pub. L. No. 88-38, 77 Stat. 56, (June 10, 1963) codified at 29 U.S.C. § 206(d), is a United States federal law amending the Fair Labor Standards Act, aimed at abolishing wage differentials based on sex. In passing the bill, Congress denounces sex discrimination.
    a. Extra time
    b. Invitee
    c. Architectural Barriers Act of 1968
    d. Equal Pay Act of 1963

3. _____ describes the situation when output from (or information about the result of) an event or phenomenon in the past will influence the same event/phenomenon in the present or future. When an event is part of a chain of cause-and-effect that forms a circuit or loop, then the event is said to 'feed back' into itself.

    _____ is also a synonym for:

    - _____ signal; the information about the initial event that is the basis for subsequent modification of the event.
    - _____ loop; the causal path that leads from the initial generation of the _____ signal to the subsequent modification of the event.

    _____ is a mechanism, process or signal that is looped back to control a system within itself. Such a loop is called a _____ loop.

    a. Feedback loop
    b. Positive feedback
    c. 1990 Clean Air Act
    d. Feedback

4. The _____ of 1990 (ADA) is the short title of United States (Pub.L. 101-336, 104 Stat. 327, enacted July 26, 1990), codified at 42 U.S.C. § 12101 et seq. It was signed into law on July 26, 1990, by President George H. W. Bush, and later amended with changes effective January 1, 2009. The ADA is a wide-ranging civil rights law that prohibits, under certain circumstances, discrimination based on disability. It affords similar protections against discrimination to Americans with disabilities as the Civil Rights Act of 1964,

a. Equal Pay Act of 1963
b. Employment discrimination
c. Americans with Disabilities Act
d. Australian labour law

5. _____ is a cross-disciplinary area concerned with protecting the safety, health and welfare of people engaged in work or employment. The goal of all _____ programs is to foster a work free safe environment. As a secondary effect, it may also protect co-workers, family members, employers, customers, suppliers, nearby communities, and other members of the public who are impacted by the workplace environment.
   a. AAAI
   b. A4e
   c. A Stake in the Outcome
   d. Occupational Safety and Health

6. The United States _____ is an agency of the United States Department of Labor. It was created by Congress under the Occupational Safety and Health Act, signed by President Richard M. Nixon, on December 29, 1970. Its mission is to prevent work-related injuries, illnesses, and deaths by issuing and enforcing rules (called standards) for workplace safety and health.
   a. Occupational Safety and Health Administration
   b. Unemployment insurance
   c. Operant conditioning
   d. Opinion leadership

7. _____ is one of the managerial functions like planning, organizing, staffing and directing. It is an important function because it helps to check the errors and to take the corrective action so that deviation from standards are minimized and stated goals of the organization are achieved in desired manner. According to modern concepts, _____ is a foreseeing action whereas earlier concept of _____ was used only when errors were detected. _____ in management means setting standards, measuring actual performance and taking corrective action.
   a. Decision tree pruning
   b. Turnover
   c. Control
   d. Schedule of reinforcement

Chapter 4. Training and Orientation

8. _____ occurs when expectant women are fired, not hired, or otherwise discriminated against due to their pregnancy or intention to become pregnant. Common forms of _____ include not being hired due to visible pregnancy or likelihood of becoming pregnant, being fired after informing an employer of one's pregnancy, being fired after maternity leave, and receiving a pay dock due to pregnancy. In the United States, since 1978, employers are legally bound to provide what insurance, leave pay, and additional support that would be bestowed upon any employee with medical leave or disability.
   a. 1990 Clean Air Act
   b. 33 Strategies of War
   c. 28-hour day
   d. Pregnancy Discrimination

9. A _____ is a list of the general tasks and responsibilities of a position. Typically, it also includes to whom the position reports, specifications such as the qualifications needed by the person in the job, salary range for the position, etc. A _____ is usually developed by conducting a job analysis, which includes examining the tasks and sequences of tasks necessary to perform the job.
   a. Recruitment advertising
   b. Job description
   c. Recruitment
   d. Recruitment Process Insourcing

10. The _____ was a landmark piece of legislation in the United States that outlawed racial segregation in schools, public places, and employment.
    a. Design patent
    b. Financial Security Law of France
    c. Civil Rights Act of 1964
    d. Negligence in employment

11. _____ is a term used to describe a policy of allowing events to take their own course. The term is a French phrase literally meaning 'let do'. It is a doctrine that states that government generally should not intervene in the marketplace.
    a. Libertarian
    b. Freedom of contract
    c. Deep ecology
    d. Laissez-faire

12. _____ has been described as the 'process of social influence in which one person can enlist the aid and support of others in the accomplishment of a common task'. A definition more inclusive of followers comes from Alan Keith of Genentech who said '_____ is ultimately about creating a way for people to contribute to making something extraordinary happen.'

_____ is one of the most salient aspects of the organizational context. However, defining _____ has been challenging.

   a. Situational leadership
   b. Leadership
   c. 28-hour day
   d. 1990 Clean Air Act

13. _____, sometimes referred to as 'cumulative causation', is a feedback loop system in which the system responds to perturbation in the same direction as the perturbation. In contrast, a system that responds to the perturbation in the opposite direction is called a negative feedback system. These concepts were first recognized as broadly applicable by Norbert Wiener in his 1948 work on cybernetics.
   a. 1990 Clean Air Act
   b. Negative feedback
   c. Feedback loop
   d. Positive feedback

14. In a human resources context, _____ or labor _____ is the rate at which an employer gains and loses employees. Simple ways to describe it are 'how long employees tend to stay' or 'the rate of traffic through the revolving door.' _____ is measured for individual companies and for their industry as a whole. If an employer is said to have a high _____ relative to its competitors, it means that employees of that company have a shorter average tenure than those of other companies in the same industry.
   a. Continuous
   b. Career portfolios
   c. Turnover
   d. Ten year occupational employment projection

15. _____ plant, and equipment, is a term used in accountancy for assets and property which cannot easily be converted into cash. This can be compared with current assets such as cash or bank accounts, which are described as liquid assets. In most cases, only tangible assets are referred to as fixed.

a. 28-hour day
b. 1990 Clean Air Act
c. 33 Strategies of War
d. Fixed asset

Chapter 5. Managing Productivity and Controlling Labor Costs

1. _____ occurs when expectant women are fired, not hired, or otherwise discriminated against due to their pregnancy or intention to become pregnant. Common forms of _____ include not being hired due to visible pregnancy or likelihood of becoming pregnant, being fired after informing an employer of one's pregnancy, being fired after maternity leave, and receiving a pay dock due to pregnancy. In the United States, since 1978, employers are legally bound to provide what insurance, leave pay, and additional support that would be bestowed upon any employee with medical leave or disability.
    a. 28-hour day
    b. 33 Strategies of War
    c. 1990 Clean Air Act
    d. Pregnancy Discrimination

2. _____ refers to metrics and measures of output from production processes, per unit of input. Labor _____, for example, is typically measured as a ratio of output per labor-hour, an input. _____ may be conceived of as a metrics of the technical or engineering efficiency of production.
    a. Value engineering
    b. Master production schedule
    c. Remanufacturing
    d. Productivity

3. _____ is a cross-disciplinary area concerned with protecting the safety, health and welfare of people engaged in work or employment. The goal of all _____ programs is to foster a work free safe environment. As a secondary effect, it may also protect co-workers, family members, employers, customers, suppliers, nearby communities, and other members of the public who are impacted by the workplace environment.
    a. AAAI
    b. Occupational Safety and Health
    c. A Stake in the Outcome
    d. A4e

4. The United States _____ is an agency of the United States Department of Labor. It was created by Congress under the Occupational Safety and Health Act, signed by President Richard M. Nixon, on December 29, 1970. Its mission is to prevent work-related injuries, illnesses, and deaths by issuing and enforcing rules (called standards) for workplace safety and health.
    a. Operant conditioning
    b. Unemployment insurance
    c. Occupational Safety and Health Administration
    d. Opinion leadership

Chapter 5. Managing Productivity and Controlling Labor Costs

5. The _____ of 1990 (ADA) is the short title of United States (Pub.L. 101-336, 104 Stat. 327, enacted July 26, 1990), codified at 42 U.S.C. Â§ 12101 et seq. It was signed into law on July 26, 1990, by President George H. W. Bush, and later amended with changes effective January 1, 2009. The ADA is a wide-ranging civil rights law that prohibits, under certain circumstances, discrimination based on disability. It affords similar protections against discrimination to Americans with disabilities as the Civil Rights Act of 1964,
   a. Australian labour law
   b. Employment discrimination
   c. Americans with Disabilities Act
   d. Equal Pay Act of 1963

6. A _____ is the belief that there is a technique, method, process, activity, incentive or reward that is more effective at delivering a particular outcome than any other technique, method, process, etc. The idea is that with proper processes, checks, and testing, a desired outcome can be delivered with fewer problems and unforeseen complications. _____s can also be defined as the most efficient (least amount of effort) and effective (best results) way of accomplishing a task, based on repeatable procedures that have proven themselves over time for large numbers of people.
   a. Best practice
   b. Fix it twice
   c. Design management
   d. Hierarchical organization

7. In economics, business, retail, and accounting, a _____ is the value of money that has been used up to produce something, and hence is not available for use anymore. In economics, a _____ is an alternative that is given up as a result of a decision. In business, the _____ may be one of acquisition, in which case the amount of money expended to acquire it is counted as _____.
   a. Cost allocation
   b. Cost
   c. Cost overrun
   d. Fixed costs

8. The _____ 1970 is an Act of the United Kingdom Parliament which prohibits any less favourable treatment between men and women in terms of pay and conditions of employment. It came into force on 29 December 1975. The term pay is interpreted in a broad sense to include, on top of wages, things like holidays, pension rights, company perks and some kinds of bonuses.
   a. Australian labour law
   b. Architectural Barriers Act of 1968
   c. Oncale v. Sundowner Offshore Services
   d. Equal Pay Act

Chapter 5. Managing Productivity and Controlling Labor Costs

9. The _____, Pub. L. No. 88-38, 77 Stat. 56, (June 10, 1963) codified at 29 U.S.C. § 206(d), is a United States federal law amending the Fair Labor Standards Act, aimed at abolishing wage differentials based on sex. In passing the bill, Congress denounces sex discrimination.
   a. Extra time
   b. Equal Pay Act of 1963
   c. Invitee
   d. Architectural Barriers Act of 1968

10. _____ is the process of estimation in unknown situations. Prediction is a similar, but more general term. Both can refer to estimation of time series, cross-sectional or longitudinal data.
    a. 1990 Clean Air Act
    b. 28-hour day
    c. 33 Strategies of War
    d. Forecasting

11. _____ is a term used to describe a policy of allowing events to take their own course. The term is a French phrase literally meaning 'let do'. It is a doctrine that states that government generally should not intervene in the marketplace.
    a. Freedom of contract
    b. Libertarian
    c. Deep ecology
    d. Laissez-faire

12. _____ has been described as the 'process of social influence in which one person can enlist the aid and support of others in the accomplishment of a common task'. A definition more inclusive of followers comes from Alan Keith of Genentech who said '_____ is ultimately about creating a way for people to contribute to making something extraordinary happen.'

    _____ is one of the most salient aspects of the organizational context. However, defining _____ has been challenging.

    a. 28-hour day
    b. Situational leadership
    c. Leadership
    d. 1990 Clean Air Act

Chapter 5. Managing Productivity and Controlling Labor Costs

13. In statistics, a _____ rolling mean or running average, is a type of finite impulse response filter used to analyze a set of data points by creating a series of averages of different subsets of the full data set. A _____ is not a single number, but it is a set of numbers, each of which is the average of the corresponding subset of a larger set of data points. A _____ may also use unequal weights for each data value in the subset to emphasize particular values in the subset.
   a. Homoscedastic
   b. Time series analysis
   c. Standard deviation
   d. Moving average

14. The _____ of 1967, Pub. L. No. 90-202, 81 Stat. 602 (Dec. 15, 1967), codified as Chapter 14 of Title 29 of the United States Code, 29 U.S.C. Â§ 621 through 29 U.S.C. Â§ 634 (ADEA), prohibits employment discrimination against persons 40 years of age or older in the United States). The law also sets standards for pensions and benefits provided by employers and requires that information about the needs of older workers be provided to the general public.
   a. Age Discrimination in Employment Act
   b. Extra time
   c. Undue hardship
   d. Unemployment and Farm Relief Act

15. The _____ was a landmark piece of legislation in the United States that outlawed racial segregation in schools, public places, and employment.
   a. Civil Rights Act of 1964
   b. Financial Security Law of France
   c. Design patent
   d. Negligence in employment

16. _____ is a contract between two parties, one being the employer and the other being the employee. An employee may be defined as: 'A person in the service of another under any contract of hire, express or implied, oral or written, where the employer has the power or right to control and direct the employee in the material details of how the work is to be performed.' Black's Law Dictionary page 471 (5th ed. 1979.)
   a. Employment counsellor
   b. Exit interview
   c. Employment
   d. Employment rate

17. _____, is an employment schedule, a type of Shift work where a person's normal work day is split in to 2 or more segments, for example a person may work from 5 a.m. to 9 a.m. and then have a break until 3 p.m. at which point they might return to work until 7 p.m.. This is especially common for public transport employees where it is advantageous to have additional staff working during traditional rush hour times and for bar staff who would work at lunch and during the evening. It is generally not a desired shift since one is basically tied to work all day, and your time in between shifts can be taken up by getting to and from work.
   a. Peak earning years
   b. Split shift
   c. Permatemp
   d. Performance improvement plan

18. _____ is one of the managerial functions like planning, organizing, staffing and directing. It is an important function because it helps to check the errors and to take the corrective action so that deviation from standards are minimized and stated goals of the organization are achieved in desired manner.According to modern concepts, _____ is a foreseeing action whereas earlier concept of _____ was used only when errors were detected. _____ in management means setting standards, measuring actual performance and taking corrective action.
   a. Schedule of reinforcement
   b. Decision tree pruning
   c. Control
   d. Turnover

19. _____ generally refers to a list of all planned expenses and revenues. It is a plan for saving and spending. A _____ is an important concept in microeconomics, which uses a _____ line to illustrate the trade-offs between two or more goods.
   a. 1990 Clean Air Act
   b. 33 Strategies of War
   c. 28-hour day
   d. Budget

Chapter 6. Evaluating and Coaching

1. _____ is a cross-disciplinary area concerned with protecting the safety, health and welfare of people engaged in work or employment. The goal of all _____ programs is to foster a work free safe environment. As a secondary effect, it may also protect co-workers, family members, employers, customers, suppliers, nearby communities, and other members of the public who are impacted by the workplace environment.
   a. AAAI
   b. A Stake in the Outcome
   c. A4e
   d. Occupational Safety and Health

2. The United States _____ is an agency of the United States Department of Labor. It was created by Congress under the Occupational Safety and Health Act, signed by President Richard M. Nixon, on December 29, 1970. Its mission is to prevent work-related injuries, illnesses, and deaths by issuing and enforcing rules (called standards) for workplace safety and health.
   a. Operant conditioning
   b. Opinion leadership
   c. Occupational Safety and Health Administration
   d. Unemployment insurance

3. The _____ 1970 is an Act of the United Kingdom Parliament which prohibits any less favourable treatment between men and women in terms of pay and conditions of employment. It came into force on 29 December 1975. The term pay is interpreted in a broad sense to include, on top of wages, things like holidays, pension rights, company perks and some kinds of bonuses.
   a. Oncale v. Sundowner Offshore Services
   b. Australian labour law
   c. Architectural Barriers Act of 1968
   d. Equal Pay Act

4. The _____, Pub. L. No. 88-38, 77 Stat. 56, (June 10, 1963) codified at 29 U.S.C. § 206(d), is a United States federal law amending the Fair Labor Standards Act, aimed at abolishing wage differentials based on sex. In passing the bill, Congress denounces sex discrimination.
   a. Invitee
   b. Equal Pay Act of 1963
   c. Architectural Barriers Act of 1968
   d. Extra time

5. _____ describes the situation when output from (or information about the result of) an event or phenomenon in the past will influence the same event/phenomenon in the present or future. When an event is part of a chain of cause-and-effect that forms a circuit or loop, then the event is said to 'feed back' into itself.

Chapter 6. Evaluating and Coaching

_____ is also a synonym for:

- _____ signal; the information about the initial event that is the basis for subsequent modification of the event.
- _____ loop; the causal path that leads from the initial generation of the _____ signal to the subsequent modification of the event.

_____ is a mechanism, process or signal that is looped back to control a system within itself. Such a loop is called a _____ loop.

a. 1990 Clean Air Act
b. Feedback loop
c. Positive feedback
d. Feedback

6. The _____ of 1990 (ADA) is the short title of United States (Pub.L. 101-336, 104 Stat. 327, enacted July 26, 1990), codified at 42 U.S.C. § 12101 et seq. It was signed into law on July 26, 1990, by President George H. W. Bush, and later amended with changes effective January 1, 2009. The ADA is a wide-ranging civil rights law that prohibits, under certain circumstances, discrimination based on disability. It affords similar protections against discrimination to Americans with disabilities as the Civil Rights Act of 1964,
   a. Americans with Disabilities Act
   b. Australian labour law
   c. Employment discrimination
   d. Equal Pay Act of 1963

7. _____ is a term used to describe a policy of allowing events to take their own course. The term is a French phrase literally meaning 'let do'. It is a doctrine that states that government generally should not intervene in the marketplace.
   a. Deep ecology
   b. Freedom of contract
   c. Laissez-faire
   d. Libertarian

8. _____ occurs when expectant women are fired, not hired, or otherwise discriminated against due to their pregnancy or intention to become pregnant. Common forms of _____ include not being hired due to visible pregnancy or likelihood of becoming pregnant, being fired after informing an employer of one's pregnancy, being fired after maternity leave, and receiving a pay dock due to pregnancy. In the United States, since 1978, employers are legally bound to provide what insurance, leave pay, and additional support that would be bestowed upon any employee with medical leave or disability.

Chapter 6. Evaluating and Coaching

a. 1990 Clean Air Act
b. 28-hour day
c. Pregnancy Discrimination
d. 33 Strategies of War

9. The _____ refers to a cognitive bias whereby the perception of a particular trait is influenced by the perception of the former traits in a sequence of interpretations.

Edward L. Thorndike was the first to support the _____ with empirical research. In a psychology study published in 1920, Thorndike asked commanding officers to rate their soldiers; Thorndike found high cross-correlation between all positive and all negative traits.

a. Halo effect
b. Distinction bias
c. Sunk costs
d. Cognitive biases

10. _____ has been described as the 'process of social influence in which one person can enlist the aid and support of others in the accomplishment of a common task'. A definition more inclusive of followers comes from Alan Keith of Genentech who said '_____ is ultimately about creating a way for people to contribute to making something extraordinary happen.'

_____ is one of the most salient aspects of the organizational context. However, defining _____ has been challenging.

a. 1990 Clean Air Act
b. 28-hour day
c. Leadership
d. Situational leadership

11. The _____ of 1967, Pub. L. No. 90-202, 81 Stat. 602 (Dec. 15, 1967), codified as Chapter 14 of Title 29 of the United States Code, 29 U.S.C. § 621 through 29 U.S.C. § 634 (ADEA), prohibits employment discrimination against persons 40 years of age or older in the United States). The law also sets standards for pensions and benefits provided by employers and requires that information about the needs of older workers be provided to the general public.

a. Undue hardship
b. Unemployment and Farm Relief Act
c. Extra time
d. Age Discrimination in Employment Act

Chapter 6. Evaluating and Coaching

12. The _____ was a landmark piece of legislation in the United States that outlawed racial segregation in schools, public places, and employment.
    a. Negligence in employment
    b. Financial Security Law of France
    c. Civil Rights Act of 1964
    d. Design patent

13. _____ is a contract between two parties, one being the employer and the other being the employee. An employee may be defined as: 'A person in the service of another under any contract of hire, express or implied, oral or written, where the employer has the power or right to control and direct the employee in the material details of how the work is to be performed.' Black's Law Dictionary page 471 (5th ed. 1979.)
    a. Employment rate
    b. Exit interview
    c. Employment
    d. Employment counsellor

14. _____ is one of the four elements of marketing mix. An organization or set of organizations (go-betweens) involved in the process of making a product or service available for use or consumption by a consumer or business user.

    The other three parts of the marketing mix are product, pricing, and promotion.

    a. Job creation programs
    b. Matching theory
    c. Missing completely at random
    d. Distribution

15. _____ consists of the mental process of thinking involved with the process of judging the merits of multiple options and selecting one of them for action. Some simple examples include deciding whether to get up in the morning or go back to sleep, or selecting a given route for a journey. More complex examples (often decisions that affect what a person thinks or their core beliefs) include choosing a lifestyle, religious affiliation, or political position.
    a. Trade study
    b. Championship mobilization
    c. Choice
    d. Groups decision making

16. A _____ is a set of categories designed to elicit information about a quantitative or a qualitative attribute. In the social sciences, common examples are the Likert scale and 1-10 _____s in which a person selects the number which is considered to reflect the perceived quality of a product.

A _____ is an instrument that requires the rater to assign the rated object that have numerals assigned to them.

a. Thurstone scale
b. Polytomous Rasch model
c. Spearman-Brown prediction formula
d. Rating scale

17. _____ is a process of agreeing upon objectives within an organization so that management and employees agree to the objectives and understand what they are in the organization.

The term '_____' was first popularized by Peter Drucker in his 1954 book 'The Practice of Management'.

The essence of _____ is participative goal setting, choosing course of actions and decision making.

a. Business economics
b. Management by objectives
c. Clean sheet review
d. Job enrichment

18. _____ is one of the managerial functions like planning, organizing, staffing and directing. It is an important function because it helps to check the errors and to take the corrective action so that deviation from standards are minimized and stated goals of the organization are achieved in desired manner. According to modern concepts, _____ is a foreseeing action whereas earlier concept of _____ was used only when errors were detected. _____ in management means setting standards, measuring actual performance and taking corrective action.

a. Schedule of reinforcement
b. Control
c. Turnover
d. Decision tree pruning

Chapter 7. Discipline

1. The _____ was a landmark piece of legislation in the United States that outlawed racial segregation in schools, public places, and employment.
   a. Financial Security Law of France
   b. Design patent
   c. Negligence in employment
   d. Civil Rights Act of 1964

2. _____ is a cross-disciplinary area concerned with protecting the safety, health and welfare of people engaged in work or employment. The goal of all _____ programs is to foster a work free safe environment. As a secondary effect, it may also protect co-workers, family members, employers, customers, suppliers, nearby communities, and other members of the public who are impacted by the workplace environment.
   a. A4e
   b. AAAI
   c. A Stake in the Outcome
   d. Occupational Safety and Health

3. The United States _____ is an agency of the United States Department of Labor. It was created by Congress under the Occupational Safety and Health Act, signed by President Richard M. Nixon, on December 29, 1970. Its mission is to prevent work-related injuries, illnesses, and deaths by issuing and enforcing rules (called standards) for workplace safety and health.
   a. Unemployment insurance
   b. Opinion leadership
   c. Operant conditioning
   d. Occupational Safety and Health Administration

4. In operant conditioning, _____ occurs when an event following a response causes an increase in the probability of that response occurring in the future. Response strength can be assessed by measures such as the frequency with which the response is made (for example, a pigeon may peck a key more times in the session), or the speed with which it is made (for example, a rat may run a maze faster.) The environment change contingent upon the response is called a reinforcer.
   a. Reinforcement
   b. Diminishing Manufacturing Sources and Material Shortages
   c. Meetings, Incentives, Conferences, and Exhibitions
   d. Historiometry

Chapter 7. Discipline

5. _____ occurs when expectant women are fired, not hired, or otherwise discriminated against due to their pregnancy or intention to become pregnant. Common forms of _____ include not being hired due to visible pregnancy or likelihood of becoming pregnant, being fired after informing an employer of one's pregnancy, being fired after maternity leave, and receiving a pay dock due to pregnancy. In the United States, since 1978, employers are legally bound to provide what insurance, leave pay, and additional support that would be bestowed upon any employee with medical leave or disability.
   a. 1990 Clean Air Act
   b. 28-hour day
   c. Pregnancy Discrimination
   d. 33 Strategies of War

6. _____ is a system of discipline where the penalties increase upon repeat occurrences.

This term is often used in an employment or human resources context where rather than terminating employees for first or minor infractions, there is a system of escalating responses intended to correct the negative behaviour rather than to punish the employee.

The typical stages of _____ in a workplace are:

   1. Counselling or a verbal warning;
   2. A written warning;
   3. Suspension or demotion; and
   4. Termination.

The stage chosen for a particular infraction will depend on a variety of factors that include the severity of the infraction, the previous work history of the employee and how the choice will affect others in the organization.

   a. Progressive discipline
   b. Salary
   c. Performance appraisal
   d. Human resource management

7. _____ is a term used to describe a policy of allowing events to take their own course. The term is a French phrase literally meaning 'let do'. It is a doctrine that states that government generally should not intervene in the marketplace.
   a. Freedom of contract
   b. Laissez-faire
   c. Deep ecology
   d. Libertarian

8. _____ has been described as the 'process of social influence in which one person can enlist the aid and support of others in the accomplishment of a common task' . A definition more inclusive of followers comes from Alan Keith of Genentech who said '_____ is ultimately about creating a way for people to contribute to making something extraordinary happen.'

_____ is one of the most salient aspects of the organizational context. However, defining _____ has been challenging.

   a. Situational leadership
   b. Leadership
   c. 28-hour day
   d. 1990 Clean Air Act

Chapter 8. Special Supervisory Concerns

1. The _____ was a landmark piece of legislation in the United States that outlawed racial segregation in schools, public places, and employment.
   a. Civil Rights Act of 1964
   b. Negligence in employment
   c. Financial Security Law of France
   d. Design patent

2. _____ is a contract between two parties, one being the employer and the other being the employee. An employee may be defined as: 'A person in the service of another under any contract of hire, express or implied, oral or written, where the employer has the power or right to control and direct the employee in the material details of how the work is to be performed.' Black's Law Dictionary page 471 (5th ed. 1979.)
   a. Employment counsellor
   b. Employment rate
   c. Employment
   d. Exit interview

3. The term _____ was created by President Lyndon B. Johnson when he signed Executive Order 11246 on September 24, 1965, created to prohibit federal contractors from discriminating against employees on the basis of race, sex, creed, religion, color, or national origin. In more recent times, most employers have also added sexual orientation to the list of non-discrimination.

   The Executive Order also required contractors to implement affirmative action plans to increase the participation of minorities and women in the workplace.

   a. A Stake in the Outcome
   b. A4e
   c. Equal employment opportunity
   d. AAAI

4. The _____ of 1990 (ADA) is the short title of United States (Pub.L. 101-336, 104 Stat. 327, enacted July 26, 1990), codified at 42 U.S.C. § 12101 et seq. It was signed into law on July 26, 1990, by President George H. W. Bush, and later amended with changes effective January 1, 2009. The ADA is a wide-ranging civil rights law that prohibits, under certain circumstances, discrimination based on disability. It affords similar protections against discrimination to Americans with disabilities as the Civil Rights Act of 1964,
   a. Equal Pay Act of 1963
   b. Employment discrimination
   c. Americans with Disabilities Act
   d. Australian labour law

Chapter 8. Special Supervisory Concerns

5. In employment law, a (BFOQ) (US) or bona fide occupational requirement (BFOR) (Canada) is a quality or an attribute that employers are allowed to consider when making decisions on the hiring and retention of employees - qualities that, when considered, in other contexts would be considered discriminatory and thus violating civil rights employment law.

In employment discrimination law in the United States, United States Code Title 29, Chapter 14 (age discrimination in employment), section 623 (prohibition of age discrimination) establishes that 'It shall not be unlawful for an employer, employment agency, or labor organization (1) to take any action otherwise prohibited under subsections (a), (b), (c), or (e) of this section where age is a _____ reasonably necessary to the normal operation of the particular business, or where the differentiation is based on reasonable factors other than age, or where such practices involve an employee in a workplace in a foreign country, and compliance with such subsections would cause such employer, or a corporation controlled by such employer, to violate the laws of the country in which such workplace is located.'

One example of _____s are mandatory retirement ages for bus drivers and airline pilots, for safety reasons. Further, in advertising, a manufacturer of men's clothing may lawfully advertise for male models.

   a. Corporate governance
   b. Bona fide occupational qualification
   c. Sick leave
   d. MacPherson v. Buick Motor Co.

6. The _____ of 1967, Pub. L. No. 90-202, 81 Stat. 602 (Dec. 15, 1967), codified as Chapter 14 of Title 29 of the United States Code, 29 U.S.C. § 621 through 29 U.S.C. § 634 (ADEA), prohibits employment discrimination against persons 40 years of age or older in the United States). The law also sets standards for pensions and benefits provided by employers and requires that information about the needs of older workers be provided to the general public.
   a. Unemployment and Farm Relief Act
   b. Age Discrimination in Employment Act
   c. Undue hardship
   d. Extra time

7. The _____ 1970 is an Act of the United Kingdom Parliament which prohibits any less favourable treatment between men and women in terms of pay and conditions of employment. It came into force on 29 December 1975. The term pay is interpreted in a broad sense to include, on top of wages, things like holidays, pension rights, company perks and some kinds of bonuses.
   a. Equal Pay Act
   b. Australian labour law
   c. Oncale v. Sundowner Offshore Services
   d. Architectural Barriers Act of 1968

Chapter 8. Special Supervisory Concerns

8. The _____, Pub. L. No. 88-38, 77 Stat. 56, (June 10, 1963) codified at 29 U.S.C. § 206(d), is a United States federal law amending the Fair Labor Standards Act, aimed at abolishing wage differentials based on sex. In passing the bill, Congress denounces sex discrimination.
   a. Architectural Barriers Act of 1968
   b. Extra time
   c. Invitee
   d. Equal Pay Act of 1963

9. _____ occurs when expectant women are fired, not hired, or otherwise discriminated against due to their pregnancy or intention to become pregnant. Common forms of _____ include not being hired due to visible pregnancy or likelihood of becoming pregnant, being fired after informing an employer of one's pregnancy, being fired after maternity leave, and receiving a pay dock due to pregnancy. In the United States, since 1978, employers are legally bound to provide what insurance, leave pay, and additional support that would be bestowed upon any employee with medical leave or disability.
   a. 33 Strategies of War
   b. 28-hour day
   c. 1990 Clean Air Act
   d. Pregnancy Discrimination

10. The _____ of 1938 (_____, ch. 676, 52 Stat. 1060, June 25, 1938, 29 U.S.C. ch.8), also called the Wages and Hours Bill, is United States federal law that applies to employees engaged in interstate commerce or employed by an enterprise engaged in commerce or in the production of goods for commerce, unless the employer can claim an exemption from coverage. The _____ established a national minimum wage, guaranteed time and a half for overtime in certain jobs, and prohibited most employment of minors in 'oppressive child labor,' a term defined in the statute.
    a. Family and Medical Leave Act of 1993
    b. Fair Labor Standards Act
    c. Board of directors
    d. Joint venture

11. The _____ is a United States labor law allowing an employee to take unpaid leave due to a serious health condition that makes the employee unable to perform his job or to care for a sick family member or to care for a new son or daughter (including by birth, adoption or foster care.) The bill was among the first signed into law by President Bill Clinton in his first term.
    a. Contributory negligence
    b. Sarbanes-Oxley Act of 2002
    c. Harvester Judgment
    d. Family and Medical Leave Act of 1993

Chapter 8. Special Supervisory Concerns

12. _____ are conventions, treaties and recommendations designed to eliminate unjust and inhumane labour practices. The primary inernational agency charged with developing such standards is the International Labour Organization (ILO.) Established in 1919, the ILO advocates international standards as essential for the eradication of labour conditions involving 'injustice, hardship and privation'.
    a. International labour standards
    b. Anaconda Copper
    c. Airbus Industrie
    d. Airbus SAS

13. _____ is a term used to describe a policy of allowing events to take their own course. The term is a French phrase literally meaning 'let do'. It is a doctrine that states that government generally should not intervene in the marketplace.
    a. Libertarian
    b. Deep ecology
    c. Freedom of contract
    d. Laissez-faire

14. _____ is a cross-disciplinary area concerned with protecting the safety, health and welfare of people engaged in work or employment. The goal of all _____ programs is to foster a work free safe environment. As a secondary effect, it may also protect co-workers, family members, employers, customers, suppliers, nearby communities, and other members of the public who are impacted by the workplace environment.
    a. A Stake in the Outcome
    b. A4e
    c. AAAI
    d. Occupational Safety and Health

15. The United States _____ is an agency of the United States Department of Labor. It was created by Congress under the Occupational Safety and Health Act, signed by President Richard M. Nixon, on December 29, 1970. Its mission is to prevent work-related injuries, illnesses, and deaths by issuing and enforcing rules (called standards) for workplace safety and health.
    a. Unemployment insurance
    b. Operant conditioning
    c. Occupational Safety and Health Administration
    d. Opinion leadership

Chapter 8. Special Supervisory Concerns

16. _____ has been described as the 'process of social influence in which one person can enlist the aid and support of others in the accomplishment of a common task' . A definition more inclusive of followers comes from Alan Keith of Genentech who said '_____ is ultimately about creating a way for people to contribute to making something extraordinary happen.'

_____ is one of the most salient aspects of the organizational context. However, defining _____ has been challenging.

 a. 1990 Clean Air Act
 b. Situational leadership
 c. 28-hour day
 d. Leadership

17. A _____ is the lowest hourly, daily or monthly wage that employers may legally pay to employees or workers. Equivalently, it is the lowest wage at which workers may sell their labor. Although _____ laws are in effect in a great many jurisdictions, there are differences of opinion about the benefits and drawbacks of a _____.
 a. Deregulation
 b. Rehn-Meidner Model
 c. Value added
 d. Minimum wage

18. _____ is the amount of time someone works beyond normal working hours. Normal hours may be determined in several ways:

- by custom (what is considered healthy or reasonable by society),
- by practices of a given trade or profession,
- by legislation,
- by agreement between employers and workers or their representatives.

Most nations have _____ laws designed to dissuade or prevent employers from forcing their employees to work excessively long hours. These laws may take into account other considerations than the humanitarian, such as increasing the overall level of employment in the economy. One common approach to regulating _____ is to require employers to pay workers at a higher hourly rate for _____ work.

 a. Organizational structure
 b. Industrial relations
 c. Organizational effectiveness
 d. Overtime

19. A _____ is a compensation, usually financial, received by a worker in exchange for their labor.

Chapter 8. Special Supervisory Concerns

Compensation in terms of _____s is given to worker and compensation in terms of salary is given to employees. Compensation is a monetary benefits given to employees in returns of the services provided by them.

a. Profit-sharing agreement
b. Performance-related pay
c. State Compensation Insurance Fund
d. Wage

20. _____ is unwelcome harassment of a sexual nature, or based upon the receiving party's sex or gender. In some contexts or circumstances, _____ may be illegal. It includes a range of behavior from seemingly mild transgressions and annoyances to actual sexual abuse or sexual assault.
a. 28-hour day
b. Hypernorms
c. Sexual harassment
d. 1990 Clean Air Act

21. The 'business case for _____', theorizes that in a global marketplace, a company that employs a diverse workforce (both men and women, people of many generations, people from ethnically and racially diverse backgrounds etc.) is better able to understand the demographics of the marketplace it serves and is thus better equipped to thrive in that marketplace than a company that has a more limited range of employee demographics.

An additional corollary suggests that a company that supports the _____ of its workforce can also improve employee satisfaction, productivity and retention.

a. Virtual team
b. Diversity
c. Trademark
d. Kanban

22. A _____ or labor union is an organization of workers who have banded together to achieve common goals in key areas and working conditions. The _____, through its leadership, bargains with the employer on behalf of union members (rank and file members) and negotiates labor contracts (Collective bargaining) with employers. This may include the negotiation of wages, work rules, complaint procedures, rules governing hiring, firing and promotion of workers, benefits, workplace safety and policies.

Chapter 8. Special Supervisory Concerns

a. Company union
b. Working time
c. Labour law
d. Trade union

23. In organized labor, _____ is the method whereby workers organize together (usually in unions) to meet, converse, and negotiate upon the work conditions with their employers normally resulting in a written contract setting forth the wages, hours, and other conditions to be observed for a stipulated period. It is the practice in which union and company representatives meet to negotiate a new labor contract. In various national labor and employment law contexts, the term _____ takes on a more specific legal meaning. In a broad sense, however, it is the coming together of workers to negotiate their employment.
    a. Paid time off
    b. Labour law
    c. Labor rights
    d. Collective bargaining

24. _____, a form of alternative dispute resolution (ADR), is a legal technique for the resolution of disputes outside the courts, wherein the parties to a dispute refer it to one or more persons (the 'arbitrators', 'arbiters' or 'arbitral tribunal'), by whose decision (the 'award') they agree to be bound. It is a settlement technique in which a third party reviews the case and imposes a decision that is legally binding for both sides. Other forms of ADR include mediation (a form of settlement negotiation facilitated by a neutral third party) and non-binding resolution by experts.
    a. A Stake in the Outcome
    b. A4e
    c. AAAI
    d. Arbitration

25. _____, a form of alternative dispute resolution (ADR) or 'appropriate dispute resolution', aims to assist two (or more) disputants in reaching an agreement. The parties themselves determine the conditions of any settlements reached-- rather than accepting something imposed by a third party. The disputes may involve (as parties) states, organizations, communities, individuals or other representatives with a vested interest in the outcome.
    a. Mediation
    b. Maximum medical improvement
    c. Meritor Savings Bank v. Vinson
    d. Foreign Corrupt Practices Act

Chapter 9. Team Building

1. _____ occurs when expectant women are fired, not hired, or otherwise discriminated against due to their pregnancy or intention to become pregnant. Common forms of _____ include not being hired due to visible pregnancy or likelihood of becoming pregnant, being fired after informing an employer of one's pregnancy, being fired after maternity leave, and receiving a pay dock due to pregnancy. In the United States, since 1978, employers are legally bound to provide what insurance, leave pay, and additional support that would be bestowed upon any employee with medical leave or disability.
    a. 1990 Clean Air Act
    b. 28-hour day
    c. 33 Strategies of War
    d. Pregnancy Discrimination

2. _____ is one of the managerial functions like planning, organizing, staffing and directing. It is an important function because it helps to check the errors and to take the corrective action so that deviation from standards are minimized and stated goals of the organization are achieved in desired manner. According to modern concepts, _____ is a foreseeing action whereas earlier concept of _____ was used only when errors were detected. _____ in management means setting standards, measuring actual performance and taking corrective action.
    a. Decision tree pruning
    b. Schedule of reinforcement
    c. Turnover
    d. Control

3. _____ is a term used to describe a policy of allowing events to take their own course. The term is a French phrase literally meaning 'let do'. It is a doctrine that states that government generally should not intervene in the marketplace.
    a. Libertarian
    b. Deep ecology
    c. Freedom of contract
    d. Laissez-faire

4. _____ has been described as the 'process of social influence in which one person can enlist the aid and support of others in the accomplishment of a common task' . A definition more inclusive of followers comes from Alan Keith of Genentech who said '_____ is ultimately about creating a way for people to contribute to making something extraordinary happen.'

_____ is one of the most salient aspects of the organizational context. However, defining _____ has been challenging.

a. Situational leadership
b. 28-hour day
c. Leadership
d. 1990 Clean Air Act

5. The _____ was a landmark piece of legislation in the United States that outlawed racial segregation in schools, public places, and employment.
a. Civil Rights Act of 1964
b. Financial Security Law of France
c. Design patent
d. Negligence in employment

6. _____ is a concept in ethics with several meanings. It is often used synonymously with such concepts as responsibility, answerability, enforcement, blameworthiness, liability and other terms associated with the expectation of account-giving. As an aspect of governance, it has been central to discussions related to problems in both the public and private (corporation) worlds.
a. A4e
b. A Stake in the Outcome
c. Usury
d. Accountability

7. The _____ 1970 is an Act of the United Kingdom Parliament which prohibits any less favourable treatment between men and women in terms of pay and conditions of employment. It came into force on 29 December 1975. The term pay is interpreted in a broad sense to include, on top of wages, things like holidays, pension rights, company perks and some kinds of bonuses.
a. Oncale v. Sundowner Offshore Services
b. Equal Pay Act
c. Australian labour law
d. Architectural Barriers Act of 1968

8. The _____, Pub. L. No. 88-38, 77 Stat. 56, (June 10, 1963) codified at 29 U.S.C. § 206(d), is a United States federal law amending the Fair Labor Standards Act, aimed at abolishing wage differentials based on sex. In passing the bill, Congress denounces sex discrimination.

a. Equal Pay Act of 1963
b. Invitee
c. Extra time
d. Architectural Barriers Act of 1968

9. _____ is a cross-disciplinary area concerned with protecting the safety, health and welfare of people engaged in work or employment. The goal of all _____ programs is to foster a work free safe environment. As a secondary effect, it may also protect co-workers, family members, employers, customers, suppliers, nearby communities, and other members of the public who are impacted by the workplace environment.
   a. AAAI
   b. A Stake in the Outcome
   c. A4e
   d. Occupational Safety and Health

10. The United States _____ is an agency of the United States Department of Labor. It was created by Congress under the Occupational Safety and Health Act, signed by President Richard M. Nixon, on December 29, 1970. Its mission is to prevent work-related injuries, illnesses, and deaths by issuing and enforcing rules (called standards) for workplace safety and health.
   a. Opinion leadership
   b. Unemployment insurance
   c. Operant conditioning
   d. Occupational Safety and Health Administration

11. '_____' refers to mental and communicative algorithms applied during social communications and interactions in order to reach certain effects or results. The term '_____' is used often in business contexts to refer to the measure of a person's ability to operate within business organizations through social communication and interactions. _____ are how people relate to one another.
   a. A Stake in the Outcome
   b. A4e
   c. Interpersonal skills
   d. AAAI

12. _____ of the learning curve effect and the closely related experience curve effect express the relationship between equations for experience and efficiency or between efficiency gains and investment in the effort. The experience of 'learning curves' was first observed by the 19th Century German psychologist Hermann Ebbinghaus according to the difficulty of memorizing varying numbers of verbal stimuli, and subsequent learning about the complex processes of learning are discussed in the

The rule used for representing the learning curve effect states that the more times a task has been performed, the less time will be required on each subsequent iteration.

a. Point biserial correlation coefficient
b. Models
c. Distribution
d. Spatial Decision Support Systems

13. In the social psychology of groups, _____ is the phenomenon of people making less effort to achieve a goal when they work in a group than when they work alone. This is seen as one of the main reasons groups are sometimes less productive than the combined performance of their members working as individuals.

- Ringelmann, Max : 1913

Research began in 1913 with Max Ringelmann's study. He found that when he asked a group of men to pull on a rope, that they did not pull as hard, or put as much effort into the activity, as they did when they were pulling alone.

a. Machiavellianism
b. Personal space
c. Self-enhancement
d. Social loafing

Chapter 10. Motivation Through Leadership

1. The _____ was a landmark piece of legislation in the United States that outlawed racial segregation in schools, public places, and employment.
   a. Design patent
   b. Negligence in employment
   c. Financial Security Law of France
   d. Civil Rights Act of 1964

2. _____ is a term used to describe a policy of allowing events to take their own course. The term is a French phrase literally meaning 'let do'. It is a doctrine that states that government generally should not intervene in the marketplace.
   a. Deep ecology
   b. Libertarian
   c. Laissez-faire
   d. Freedom of contract

3. _____ is a cross-disciplinary area concerned with protecting the safety, health and welfare of people engaged in work or employment. The goal of all _____ programs is to foster a work free safe environment. As a secondary effect, it may also protect co-workers, family members, employers, customers, suppliers, nearby communities, and other members of the public who are impacted by the workplace environment.
   a. AAAI
   b. A Stake in the Outcome
   c. Occupational Safety and Health
   d. A4e

4. The United States _____ is an agency of the United States Department of Labor. It was created by Congress under the Occupational Safety and Health Act, signed by President Richard M. Nixon, on December 29, 1970. Its mission is to prevent work-related injuries, illnesses, and deaths by issuing and enforcing rules (called standards) for workplace safety and health.
   a. Operant conditioning
   b. Opinion leadership
   c. Unemployment insurance
   d. Occupational Safety and Health Administration

5. _____ refers to increasing the spiritual, political, social or economic strength of individuals and communities. It often involves the empowered developing confidence in their own capacities.

The term Human _____ covers a vast landscape of meanings, interpretations, definitions and disciplines ranging from psychology and philosophy to the highly commercialized Self-Help industry and Motivational sciences.

a. AAAI
b. Empowerment
c. A Stake in the Outcome
d. A4e

6. _____ has been described as the 'process of social influence in which one person can enlist the aid and support of others in the accomplishment of a common task'. A definition more inclusive of followers comes from Alan Keith of Genentech who said '_____ is ultimately about creating a way for people to contribute to making something extraordinary happen.'

_____ is one of the most salient aspects of the organizational context. However, defining _____ has been challenging.

a. 1990 Clean Air Act
b. Situational leadership
c. 28-hour day
d. Leadership

7. _____ occurs when expectant women are fired, not hired, or otherwise discriminated against due to their pregnancy or intention to become pregnant. Common forms of _____ include not being hired due to visible pregnancy or likelihood of becoming pregnant, being fired after informing an employer of one's pregnancy, being fired after maternity leave, and receiving a pay dock due to pregnancy. In the United States, since 1978, employers are legally bound to provide what insurance, leave pay, and additional support that would be bestowed upon any employee with medical leave or disability.

a. 1990 Clean Air Act
b. Pregnancy Discrimination
c. 33 Strategies of War
d. 28-hour day

8. _____ is a concept in ethics with several meanings. It is often used synonymously with such concepts as responsibility, answerability, enforcement, blameworthiness, liability and other terms associated with the expectation of account-giving. As an aspect of governance, it has been central to discussions related to problems in both the public and private (corporation) worlds.

a. A Stake in the Outcome
b. Usury
c. A4e
d. Accountability

Chapter 10. Motivation Through Leadership

9. _____ is individual power based on a high level of identification with, admiration of, or respect for the powerholder.

Nationalism, Patriotism, Celebrities and well-respected people are examples of _____ in effect.

_____ is one of the Five Bases of Social Power, as defined by Bertram Raven and his colleagues[1] in 1959.

   a. 28-hour day
   b. Referent power
   c. 33 Strategies of War
   d. 1990 Clean Air Act

10. The _____ of 1967, Pub. L. No. 90-202, 81 Stat. 602 (Dec. 15, 1967), codified as Chapter 14 of Title 29 of the United States Code, 29 U.S.C. § 621 through 29 U.S.C. § 634 (ADEA), prohibits employment discrimination against persons 40 years of age or older in the United States). The law also sets standards for pensions and benefits provided by employers and requires that information about the needs of older workers be provided to the general public.
   a. Extra time
   b. Unemployment and Farm Relief Act
   c. Undue hardship
   d. Age Discrimination in Employment Act

11. _____ is a contract between two parties, one being the employer and the other being the employee. An employee may be defined as: 'A person in the service of another under any contract of hire, express or implied, oral or written, where the employer has the power or right to control and direct the employee in the material details of how the work is to be performed.' Black's Law Dictionary page 471 (5th ed. 1979.)
   a. Employment rate
   b. Employment counsellor
   c. Employment
   d. Exit interview

12. In a human resources context, _____ or labor _____ is the rate at which an employer gains and loses employees. Simple ways to describe it are 'how long employees tend to stay' or 'the rate of traffic through the revolving door.' _____ is measured for individual companies and for their industry as a whole. If an employer is said to have a high _____ relative to its competitors, it means that employees of that company have a shorter average tenure than those of other companies in the same industry.
   a. Career portfolios
   b. Continuous
   c. Ten year occupational employment projection
   d. Turnover

13. The _____ of 1990 (ADA) is the short title of United States (Pub.L. 101-336, 104 Stat. 327, enacted July 26, 1990), codified at 42 U.S.C. Â§ 12101 et seq. It was signed into law on July 26, 1990, by President George H. W. Bush, and later amended with changes effective January 1, 2009. The ADA is a wide-ranging civil rights law that prohibits, under certain circumstances, discrimination based on disability. It affords similar protections against discrimination to Americans with disabilities as the Civil Rights Act of 1964,
   a. Equal Pay Act of 1963
   b. Employment discrimination
   c. Australian labour law
   d. Americans with Disabilities Act

14. The _____ 1970 is an Act of the United Kingdom Parliament which prohibits any less favourable treatment between men and women in terms of pay and conditions of employment. It came into force on 29 December 1975. The term pay is interpreted in a broad sense to include, on top of wages, things like holidays, pension rights, company perks and some kinds of bonuses.
   a. Australian labour law
   b. Oncale v. Sundowner Offshore Services
   c. Architectural Barriers Act of 1968
   d. Equal Pay Act

15. The _____, Pub. L. No. 88-38, 77 Stat. 56, (June 10, 1963) codified at 29 U.S.C. Â§ 206(d), is a United States federal law amending the Fair Labor Standards Act, aimed at abolishing wage differentials based on sex. In passing the bill, Congress denounces sex discrimination.
   a. Extra time
   b. Architectural Barriers Act of 1968
   c. Equal Pay Act of 1963
   d. Invitee

16. In sociology and anthropology, an action group or _____ is a group of people joined temporarily to accomplish some task or take part in some organized collective action.

As an example, imagine that in a hypothetical culture, four bridesmaids are traditionally selected to play a role in a wedding ceremony, and eligibility to be chosen as a bridesmaid is dependent on being a young, female relative of the bride. Several people may fall into this social category: they have no automatic entitlement to the role but are eligible to assume it if chosen.

a. 28-hour day
b. 1990 Clean Air Act
c. 33 Strategies of War
d. Task group

Chapter 11. Managing Conflict

1. The _____ was a landmark piece of legislation in the United States that outlawed racial segregation in schools, public places, and employment.
   a. Negligence in employment
   b. Financial Security Law of France
   c. Design patent
   d. Civil Rights Act of 1964

2. _____ is a term used to describe a policy of allowing events to take their own course. The term is a French phrase literally meaning 'let do'. It is a doctrine that states that government generally should not intervene in the marketplace.
   a. Freedom of contract
   b. Deep ecology
   c. Libertarian
   d. Laissez-faire

3. _____ has been described as the 'process of social influence in which one person can enlist the aid and support of others in the accomplishment of a common task'. A definition more inclusive of followers comes from Alan Keith of Genentech who said '_____ is ultimately about creating a way for people to contribute to making something extraordinary happen.'

   _____ is one of the most salient aspects of the organizational context. However, defining _____ has been challenging.

   a. Situational leadership
   b. Leadership
   c. 1990 Clean Air Act
   d. 28-hour day

4. In game theory, an _____ is a set of moves or strategies taken by the players, or their payoffs resulting from the actions or strategies taken by all players. The two are complementary in that given knowledge of the set of strategies of all players, the final state of the game is known, as are any relevant payoffs. In a game where chance or a random event is involved, the _____ is not known from only the set of strategies, but is only realized when the random event(s) are realized.
   a. A4e
   b. A Stake in the Outcome
   c. AAAI
   d. Outcome

5. The _____ of 1990 (ADA) is the short title of United States (Pub.L. 101-336, 104 Stat. 327, enacted July 26, 1990), codified at 42 U.S.C. § 12101 et seq. It was signed into law on July 26, 1990, by President George H. W. Bush, and later amended with changes effective January 1, 2009. The ADA is a wide-ranging civil rights law that prohibits, under certain circumstances, discrimination based on disability. It affords similar protections against discrimination to Americans with disabilities as the Civil Rights Act of 1964,

a. Employment discrimination
b. Australian labour law
c. Equal Pay Act of 1963
d. Americans with Disabilities Act

Chapter 12. Time Management

1. _____ occurs when expectant women are fired, not hired, or otherwise discriminated against due to their pregnancy or intention to become pregnant. Common forms of _____ include not being hired due to visible pregnancy or likelihood of becoming pregnant, being fired after informing an employer of one's pregnancy, being fired after maternity leave, and receiving a pay dock due to pregnancy. In the United States, since 1978, employers are legally bound to provide what insurance, leave pay, and additional support that would be bestowed upon any employee with medical leave or disability.
   a. 33 Strategies of War
   b. Pregnancy Discrimination
   c. 1990 Clean Air Act
   d. 28-hour day

2. _____ refers to a range of skills, tools, and techniques used to manage time when accomplishing specific tasks, projects and goals. This set encompass a wide scope of activities, and these include planning, allocating, setting goals, delegation, analysis of time spent, monitoring, organizing, scheduling, and prioritizing. Initially _____ referred to just business or work activities, but eventually the term broadened to include personal activities also.
   a. Formula for Change
   b. Cash cow
   c. Voice of the customer
   d. Time management

3. The _____ was a landmark piece of legislation in the United States that outlawed racial segregation in schools, public places, and employment.
   a. Financial Security Law of France
   b. Negligence in employment
   c. Design patent
   d. Civil Rights Act of 1964

4. The _____ of 1990 (ADA) is the short title of United States (Pub.L. 101-336, 104 Stat. 327, enacted July 26, 1990), codified at 42 U.S.C. Â§ 12101 et seq. It was signed into law on July 26, 1990, by President George H. W. Bush, and later amended with changes effective January 1, 2009. The ADA is a wide-ranging civil rights law that prohibits, under certain circumstances, discrimination based on disability. It affords similar protections against discrimination to Americans with disabilities as the Civil Rights Act of 1964,
   a. Employment discrimination
   b. Americans with Disabilities Act
   c. Australian labour law
   d. Equal Pay Act of 1963

5. _____ is a concept in ethics with several meanings. It is often used synonymously with such concepts as responsibility, answerability, enforcement, blameworthiness, liability and other terms associated with the expectation of account-giving. As an aspect of governance, it has been central to discussions related to problems in both the public and private (corporation) worlds.
   a. Usury
   b. A4e
   c. Accountability
   d. A Stake in the Outcome

Chapter 13. Managing Change

1. The _____ of 1990 (ADA) is the short title of United States (Pub.L. 101-336, 104 Stat. 327, enacted July 26, 1990), codified at 42 U.S.C. § 12101 et seq. It was signed into law on July 26, 1990, by President George H. W. Bush, and later amended with changes effective January 1, 2009. The ADA is a wide-ranging civil rights law that prohibits, under certain circumstances, discrimination based on disability. It affords similar protections against discrimination to Americans with disabilities as the Civil Rights Act of 1964,
   a. Employment discrimination
   b. Equal Pay Act of 1963
   c. Australian labour law
   d. Americans with Disabilities Act

2. _____ is a term used to describe a policy of allowing events to take their own course. The term is a French phrase literally meaning 'let do'. It is a doctrine that states that government generally should not intervene in the marketplace.
   a. Libertarian
   b. Deep ecology
   c. Freedom of contract
   d. Laissez-faire

3. _____ is a structured approach to transitioning individuals, teams, and organizations from a current state to a desired future state. The current definition of _____ includes both organizational _____ processes and individual _____ models, which together are used to manage the people side of change.

   A number of models are available for understanding the transitioning of individuals through the phases of _____ and strengthening organizational development initiative in both government and corporate sectors.

   a. Change management
   b. 1990 Clean Air Act
   c. 28-hour day
   d. 33 Strategies of War

4. _____ has been described as the 'process of social influence in which one person can enlist the aid and support of others in the accomplishment of a common task'. A definition more inclusive of followers comes from Alan Keith of Genentech who said '_____ is ultimately about creating a way for people to contribute to making something extraordinary happen.'

   _____ is one of the most salient aspects of the organizational context. However, defining _____ has been challenging.

a. Leadership
b. 28-hour day
c. Situational leadership
d. 1990 Clean Air Act

5. The _____ 1970 is an Act of the United Kingdom Parliament which prohibits any less favourable treatment between men and women in terms of pay and conditions of employment. It came into force on 29 December 1975. The term pay is interpreted in a broad sense to include, on top of wages, things like holidays, pension rights, company perks and some kinds of bonuses.
a. Equal Pay Act
b. Architectural Barriers Act of 1968
c. Australian labour law
d. Oncale v. Sundowner Offshore Services

6. The _____, Pub. L. No. 88-38, 77 Stat. 56, (June 10, 1963) codified at 29 U.S.C. § 206(d), is a United States federal law amending the Fair Labor Standards Act, aimed at abolishing wage differentials based on sex. In passing the bill, Congress denounces sex discrimination.
a. Extra time
b. Invitee
c. Architectural Barriers Act of 1968
d. Equal Pay Act of 1963

7. _____ occurs when expectant women are fired, not hired, or otherwise discriminated against due to their pregnancy or intention to become pregnant. Common forms of _____ include not being hired due to visible pregnancy or likelihood of becoming pregnant, being fired after informing an employer of one's pregnancy, being fired after maternity leave, and receiving a pay dock due to pregnancy. In the United States, since 1978, employers are legally bound to provide what insurance, leave pay, and additional support that would be bestowed upon any employee with medical leave or disability.
a. 28-hour day
b. 33 Strategies of War
c. Pregnancy Discrimination
d. 1990 Clean Air Act

Chapter 14. Professional Development

1. _____ occurs when expectant women are fired, not hired, or otherwise discriminated against due to their pregnancy or intention to become pregnant. Common forms of _____ include not being hired due to visible pregnancy or likelihood of becoming pregnant, being fired after informing an employer of one's pregnancy, being fired after maternity leave, and receiving a pay dock due to pregnancy. In the United States, since 1978, employers are legally bound to provide what insurance, leave pay, and additional support that would be bestowed upon any employee with medical leave or disability.
   a. 33 Strategies of War
   b. 28-hour day
   c. 1990 Clean Air Act
   d. Pregnancy Discrimination

2. _____ is a term used to describe a policy of allowing events to take their own course. The term is a French phrase literally meaning 'let do'. It is a doctrine that states that government generally should not intervene in the marketplace.
   a. Freedom of contract
   b. Deep ecology
   c. Libertarian
   d. Laissez-faire

3. _____ has been described as the 'process of social influence in which one person can enlist the aid and support of others in the accomplishment of a common task'. A definition more inclusive of followers comes from Alan Keith of Genentech who said '_____ is ultimately about creating a way for people to contribute to making something extraordinary happen.'

   _____ is one of the most salient aspects of the organizational context. However, defining _____ has been challenging.

   a. Situational leadership
   b. 28-hour day
   c. 1990 Clean Air Act
   d. Leadership

4. The _____ 1970 is an Act of the United Kingdom Parliament which prohibits any less favourable treatment between men and women in terms of pay and conditions of employment. It came into force on 29 December 1975. The term pay is interpreted in a broad sense to include, on top of wages, things like holidays, pension rights, company perks and some kinds of bonuses.

a. Australian labour law
b. Architectural Barriers Act of 1968
c. Oncale v. Sundowner Offshore Services
d. Equal Pay Act

5. The _____, Pub. L. No. 88-38, 77 Stat. 56, (June 10, 1963) codified at 29 U.S.C. § 206(d), is a United States federal law amending the Fair Labor Standards Act, aimed at abolishing wage differentials based on sex. In passing the bill, Congress denounces sex discrimination.
   a. Invitee
   b. Architectural Barriers Act of 1968
   c. Extra time
   d. Equal Pay Act of 1963

6. _____ describes the situation when output from (or information about the result of) an event or phenomenon in the past will influence the same event/phenomenon in the present or future. When an event is part of a chain of cause-and-effect that forms a circuit or loop, then the event is said to 'feed back' into itself.

_____ is also a synonym for:

- _____ signal; the information about the initial event that is the basis for subsequent modification of the event.
- _____ loop; the causal path that leads from the initial generation of the _____ signal to the subsequent modification of the event.

_____ is a mechanism, process or signal that is looped back to control a system within itself. Such a loop is called a _____ loop.

   a. Feedback
   b. Feedback loop
   c. 1990 Clean Air Act
   d. Positive feedback

7. In human resources or industrial/organizational psychology, _____' 'multisource feedback,' or 'multisource assessment,' is feedback that comes from all around an employee. '360' refers to the 360 degrees in a circle, with an individual figuratively in the center of the circle. Feedback is provided by subordinates, peers, and supervisors.

a. Revolving door syndrome
b. Personnel management
c. Job knowledge
d. 360-degree feedback

8. The _____ of 1990 (ADA) is the short title of United States (Pub.L. 101-336, 104 Stat. 327, enacted July 26, 1990), codified at 42 U.S.C. § 12101 et seq. It was signed into law on July 26, 1990, by President George H. W. Bush, and later amended with changes effective January 1, 2009. The ADA is a wide-ranging civil rights law that prohibits, under certain circumstances, discrimination based on disability. It affords similar protections against discrimination to Americans with disabilities as the Civil Rights Act of 1964,
   a. Employment discrimination
   b. Australian labour law
   c. Equal Pay Act of 1963
   d. Americans with Disabilities Act

9. _____ is one of the managerial functions like planning, organizing, staffing and directing. It is an important function because it helps to check the errors and to take the corrective action so that deviation from standards are minimized and stated goals of the organization are achieved in desired manner. According to modern concepts, _____ is a foreseeing action whereas earlier concept of _____ was used only when errors were detected. _____ in management means setting standards, measuring actual performance and taking corrective action.
   a. Turnover
   b. Control
   c. Schedule of reinforcement
   d. Decision tree pruning

ANSWER KEY

Chapter 1
    1. b   2. d   3. c   4. d   5. d   6. c   7. d   8. d   9. d   10. c
    11. a   12. d   13. d   14. c   15. a   16. d   17. b   18. a   19. b   20. b

Chapter 2
    1. d   2. d   3. c   4. d   5. b   6. d   7. a   8. c   9. c   10. d
    11. c

Chapter 3
    1. c   2. d   3. b   4. d   5. c   6. d   7. d   8. b   9. d   10. c
    11. d   12. d   13. d   14. b   15. a   16. b

Chapter 4
    1. d   2. d   3. d   4. c   5. d   6. a   7. c   8. d   9. b   10. c
    11. d   12. b   13. d   14. c   15. d

Chapter 5
    1. d   2. d   3. b   4. c   5. c   6. a   7. b   8. d   9. b   10. d
    11. d   12. c   13. d   14. a   15. a   16. c   17. b   18. c   19. d

Chapter 6
    1. d   2. c   3. d   4. b   5. d   6. a   7. c   8. c   9. a   10. c
    11. d   12. c   13. c   14. d   15. c   16. d   17. b   18. b

Chapter 7
    1. d   2. d   3. d   4. a   5. c   6. a   7. b   8. b

Chapter 8
    1. a   2. c   3. c   4. c   5. b   6. b   7. a   8. d   9. d   10. b
    11. d   12. a   13. d   14. d   15. c   16. d   17. d   18. d   19. d   20. c
    21. b   22. d   23. d   24. d   25. a

Chapter 9
    1. d   2. d   3. d   4. c   5. a   6. d   7. b   8. a   9. d   10. d
    11. c   12. b   13. d

Chapter 10
    1. d   2. c   3. c   4. d   5. b   6. d   7. b   8. d   9. b   10. d
    11. c   12. d   13. d   14. d   15. c   16. d

Chapter 11
    1. d   2. d   3. b   4. d   5. d

Chapter 12
    1. b   2. d   3. d   4. b   5. c

ANSWER KEY

Chapter 13
1. d   2. d   3. a   4. a   5. a   6. d   7. c

Chapter 14
1. d   2. d   3. d   4. d   5. d   6. a   7. d   8. d   9. b